DREAM
TO
DESTINE

DREAM
TO
DESTINE

*Believe in you and make your
dreams get manifested*

RUPAK AICH

PARTRIDGE
A Penguin Random House Company

To order additional copies of this book, contact
Partridge India
000 800 10062 62
orders.india@partridgepublishing.com

www.partridgepublishing.com/india

Contents

Preface

This book is about self mastery. It is all about how human being creates his own destiny. It is never luck or your surroundings which make your day. It is you who make your day. We, in our daily life fail and succeed. But this book will help us see failures as learning. We lose hope, but it's nothing, this book will help you to build your hopes which are never to be loosened. The rituals of life, inner strength, our upbringing......All influence our life, but the influence which you yourself can make to your life is all about mental mastery.

This book is all about how to build inner strength. How thoughts are important in our life. The world is full of abundance; the world is ready to give us whatever we want, but the art of demanding the abundance is all about Dream to Destine. Roadblocks of life are being phenomenally common in everyone's life, everyone respond as per the stimulus, but the ability to choose response is the essence of this book.

This book is helpful for all ages, this will bring thought consciousness. To enable self fulfilling prophesy is what human kind is missing today. We have everything, it is just how to fetch all in our life, is what we need to learn. We believe in tangibility. We believe what we see. This book will help enhance the capacity of seeing. We all are here with a purpose...The purpose is to be understood and lived....

IF YOU CAN DREAM YOU CAN WIN.......

Positive thought drives us to achieve self enhancement. Driving self through positive thought is all about mastery. Every chapter of this book is making that positive thinking happen. It is a deliberate attempt to repeat all steps to get that practiced.

Idea and faith talk about all. Generating idea and keeping faith in this will cross all barriers of being mediocre or acting mediocre. The essence of managing problem and joy of feeling successful is all how we learn. When you have failed several times you learn to come back. The life is all about implementation of learning and achieving self mastery. It is just bringing positive attitude in all spheres of life and practice that attitude all though.

Faith and thought really connect. This is where we actually need to concentrate. The power of attracting is all about faith. Faith help us

a. Learn to demand
b. Learn to desire
c. Learn to receive

Faith help us change, connect to source, clears our vision, establishes self confidence. Emerging life and dreams at different stages of life make us know the difficulties of dreaming. Dreams of childhood and adult do not match. If we are able to match these dreams of different phases of life, we are on the right track of achieving success. It is only belief of dream which make us succeed.

We tried to find the answer of question in this book. Who am I? We have power to choose. The power of choices creates our response. The feeling of God beside us is making us learn how to choose. Learn to choose. We see how natural laws drive us. Knowing birth intelligences make us aware how resourceful we are. Practicing those intelligences will only help us aligning with success. We will become aware of our conscious and subconscious mind. Learning to nurture subconscious mind will create good life.

Failures stop us. But failures are never final. We get stuck to manifest positive in our life, which are actually stepping stones of our success. The positives are only of omnipotence. Creating energy within will only bring positives around.

Feel the crowning of life. Its all pleasure of success. The success can be defined and achieved.

Introduction

"Destiny is no matter of chance—it is matter of choice. (William fennins Bryan- US political Leader)

Dream…..Does it make any difference! If you dream it, you can become it.

It is us who makes this world; Everybody plays a role and it is ongoing….. Destiny is never seen…but thought….thought becomes faith…..faith is the law of subconscious mind……subconscious mind help us dream…...

Your thought only drives your dream, but dreams whether good or bad are dreams only. We only make it good or bad. We distinguish the quality of dream and sometime think of or understand accountability of having good or bad dreams. Dreams are dreams which is seen when our eyes are open, not are dreams when our eyes are closed. We don't understand the origination of these, but we all are destined to make these fulfilled. Fulfilling of dream is not only striving to achieve but also preparing us to get that achieved. We human being has all potential to make this fulfilled, but the desire to achieve is the crux. We all are originated from a source, a source of abundance. The abundance is only about good. We think, we act but all of us wishes to be successful, happy and fulfilled with abundance of joy. Dreams make us go along but only few of us believe, faith turns into dreams are achievable.

Believe on dream, thinking of the source we emanate, not postponing it, only helps us to build dream and make it happen.

Happiness is not something readymade; it comes from your own deeds….

Belief, faith, positive feelings make us attracted to our source, negative feeling, hatred, fear of loss makes us away from our source. Positive actions of all thoughts make us feel contented. All of us have been given a life which is meant to be fulfilled but the differences lies in belief of individual.

Rupak Aich

Childhood, then after being adult has been a truth, but what makes us wealthy is our thoughts during the journey of life all together. We think in a set pattern in all phases of life, we behave in a style in all phases of life but the truth is we think, we act and we dream differently throughout. We only miss thinking positively. The positive thinking only makes us different. Although thinking differently do not make any sense if we do not act differently and our thought makes us different.

Our mind, conscious and subconscious, makes us feel differently. Our subconscious mind believes in principles. Law of gravity says you will always fall down from a height, whether you are good or bad. Matter expands when heated, water seeks its own level etc etc. Subconscious mind also believes in laws, theory. Principles make it work...............

Your feelings are your God --------Chanakya

We are born, grown up. Almost we learn same principles of being good, truthful, noble, faithful when we grow up. Also we learn for not being arrogant, greedy etc..etc.. but thoughts are different. Everyone does not think alike. Our thoughts create feeling. Our upbringing, referring life experiences, generally dominates thoughts and most of us tend to think bad which creates low feeling. The feelings attract similar kinds of feeling through Law of Attraction. Life is not happening to you, life is following you. Your feelings create a magnetic field, which attracts all likes. If it is good, it will attract good, if it is bad it will attract Bad.

Practicing feeling Great, feeling abundance, makes every individual separate from others. An Idea, your thoughts and your feelings determines what you want to be and what you dream to be.

Chapter 1

IDEA- IT'S INFLUENCE

Ideas are seeds of thought. One Idea in your mind is always a gift of God. We follow God's message. Occasionally we drop the idea, whichever comes to our mind, thinking of so many reasons, came from manifestations of rules, culture, etc. etc. We drop them thinking not possible. But which is not possible, may become probable is actually "Energetic Thinking".

Energetic Thinking:

It is success thinking, it is possible thinking. It is the first step to success. We get an Idea, which with all beliefs of us, brings all possibilities. Energetic Thinkers are everywhere; all of us can think in the same direction but when the thought is connected with the SOURCE, makes it powerful. Ideas should always be nurtured but not to be thrown away or reject. An Idea, a massage of God turns into faith, which establishes a connection with source. We should say, Mental Makeup, non corrugated thought process, and overall belief of the faith makes it powerful. It then gets a direction of fulfillment. The Energetic Thinking in other way make the idea happen and take a shape.

Energetic Thinkers brings possibilities in their life. Idea of achieving and or getting something may seem to be impossible at first place, even if thinking about it may not sometime help us. But it is important to reiterate that power of Faith only will turn into success.

Someone said "IMPOSSIBILITIES VANISH WHEN A MAN AND HIS GOD CONFRONTS MOUNTAIN".

Achieving something or to be more specific, thinking energetically every moment during the whole process of accomplishing the idea makes the idea fulfilled or accomplished. Manifestation of Power in thinking make the desired thing happens. The Mental Attitude of Energetic Thinking makes it happen. We sometime bring in or practice those attitudes on a daily basis to make us help think Powerfully. Looking at things with all kinds of possibilities, eradicates "im" from" impossible" and further makes it I AM POSSIBLE.

Be Aware- Bring in all positive attitude towards yourself:

Correcting yourself every moment with a thought process of improvement of some shortcomings, regular beliefs makes us a EnergeticThinker. We can look into our fears and develop strong will to overcome it. Think of God, who is always with us, helping us move being alongside, we can respect ourselves by respecting God and can get away with all negative thoughts, think self respected.

We can come out of thinking pathetic of any kind and always can refrain ourselves fighting negative which surely will discourage us. It is just a thought process which has to be relooked. Replacing good thoughts with bad ones are very simple to practice but of course with an intention to replace will help us doing so always.

Achievement- a feeling of completeness- becomes complete by adapting that positive attitude and simultaneously feeling of achievement will manifest. Self image; self esteem; knowing yourself, if at all you are aware; holding that high esteem is very tough always. Thinking always good is a practice by heart, thinking top of the world even if with a scratch on the body is tough, but human kind if at all want to be good can be good only by saying himself, "I am perfect". Tragic incidents make us down, faults make us realize the mistakes, sins are never forgotten; we find self esteem- a toughest ever milestone to reach. We get encouraged with even positive strokes and simultaneously we become excited and think it is simply happened by chance. This is where human being is failed to achieve that self wisdom which God has given him as a birth right. We always fail to know each one of us, we keep ourselves busy to know others and find faults in them and keep us busy comparing. We always neglect knowing us, we always wish that all our dreams to get fulfilled, even if without being attached to it.

We have a normal tendency of presenting exaggerated self shortcomings and loved to be talked about it in different occasions and try to get sympathy. Which gives us a feeling of helplessness and we could never do anything about it. But Energetic Thinkers always "CAN". They can do things, they can make think himself best in all areas. Thinking Good brings us Good. Positive self image, thinking powerfully and making all impossible to PROBABLES brings in self thinking efficiency and you bring all positive outcome in your life.

<u>Be aware to get positive attitude for attaining self Leadership</u>

Thinking excellent, good, about self is seldom seen in people but also we know that it is never absent in people. These are unseen areas, which are never thought. But Energetic Thinkers leads his life towards attaining perfection and of course drives it through inner feeling of awareness.

"Awareness precedes CHOICE and choice precedes RESULT"

You can now make choices and determine results. Prediction of positive results is very simple, only make yourself believe that result. You can think resolving problems differently. Your problems, your worries are best teacher. These always make us think differently. There is no set rule or theory of resolving problems. We always tend to look towards customary solutions of almost all problems. If something seems to be beyond our control, we raise our hand and say to us….not my cup of tea, it has to be solved by x…y…z. Coming out of Myths, beliefs, set rules of seeing things is what makes us hero. If everyone in this world is happy, the world wouldn't have given us HEROS. We only drag us behind with all kind of impossible thinking.

Self leadership is always "lead by example". Example of Good, our positive thought brings those Good to us makes us self leader. Self leaders' relish those sacrifices which has helped them think differently and attain Mental Mastery. Mastery of improving yourself every single day will bring that crown of success.

People LAZY always search COMFORT. People injured always would likely to be EMPATHETIC. Foolish people always tends to DELAY, In secured people love to be in DEEP SLEEP.

Self leadership can only help us look beyond and can make us say, WOW I have achieved ....I have completed. The belief of accomplishing targets is always relished since they have self belief.

Today's decision are tomorrow's realities. We only make us leaders, choice is with us...whether we would like to be powerful or mediocre.

Bring Positive Attitude Towards Changes:

Change is constant of life, it is fact of life, truth of Universe. Cells of our body gets changed everyday, we are a different person every day. Change is a gift of nature, brings in equilibrium. We, human beings resist it occasionally. We close our eyes and think all surroundings are in same state. We sleep opening our eyes and feel contended. We hear; i)"I am sorry, can't serve this way", ii)"Your kids are spoiled, they can never change"; iii) 'My partner can never change, it's foolish to ask change in him". One thing is very common of these thinking, it is simple ignorance of biggest truth of life "CHANGE".

Energetic thinkers adapt change, every time, everyday. Not adapting change, procrastinate the thought process of adaptability is actually a disease. This is how days slips into months and months into years. Change is the basis of hope, it is not a threat. Loving something actually will start that thing loving you. It happened with me, being very poor in public speaking since childhood, I started loving that and tried and created love for orating abilities and it has amazingly shown result and started loving me. I could understand that loving which creates irritation will certainly bring change in you and you are on the path of success.

We are generally resistant to change; it is because of contemplation of some rules which had been tought to us since childhood by our society, our surroundings, our family. We know some thumb rules of living life, and in due course of time those rules become driving factors of our thinking mechanism. It is resistance of subconscious mind which of course governed by a law of defence mechanism. It always hinders for being a positive thinker. We create impossibility in almost everything. This thought is nothing but outcome of our learnings, beliefs, seen. But one thing is very important in this, the development of beliefs— by being in the family, all we learnt is just as per process of learning but those are not rules, those are certain way to lead life without attracting change into life. People who think differently are heros and please remember mediocre thinking will only add one number in the list of followers but will not create heros.

Energetic thinkers' belief in the statement:

"Change, the way you look at things, you look at things change". It is only about seeing things differently. We are always fault finders, we never catch people doing right, and hence we always hinder people doing differently and rather drag them to think orthodox.

Bring Positive Attitude Towards Problems

Problems, challenges are another side of coin where opportunity resides. We think of problems or hindrances as reasons of being failure, and failure is always cursed. But failure is never ending. "Nobody is total failure if he dares to try something worthwhile".

You are always improved if you have crossed your yesterday's benchmark of self mastery. Never let a problem become an excuse. Think within, that a problem can never be underestimated. Take your problems seriously. "You drink a lot, but need not to worry of being suffered by lever failure"—these are dangerous thinking. You have to see this problems or bad habits seriously and obtain a solution which will determine the outcome.

Problems are milestones to be crossed over. Thinking too much or getting influenced through problems is another disaster. Someone may loose one limb in an accident but it is not the end of life since he she has his brain intact, eyes intact which is still useful, but making that remaining useful is being positive towards your problems. Someone may loose his job but that's not the end of world but a prayer and strong belief of self can make us come out since the problem is from God and solution will be from him, for sure.

You are only one responsible for managing your problem, no one will come and resolve it on your behalf. We may think, we have taken enough measures to get rid of the problem but let us wait for the right time to come out of it. The right time will never come, you searched your soul mate and love and wait for someone to come and settle both of you together, will never happen. It is you who should be doing it and remember, failures are indices of success.

"you don't win if you never begin"- waiting for the problem getting resolved thru some external help is another challenge of our thought process. Shake away your all thoughts of waiting, procrastinating; get up and take up the problem. You can see the solution just behind the wall of problem. Always think the joy we get after getting the problem resolved proactively. The delight of being self satisfied is a feeling make you top of the world. Once Nelson Mandela expressed:

"After climbing a great hill one finds there are many more hills to climb"---

problems are only stairs which helps us climb up.

Freedom only comes with responsibilities- power thinkers see problems as opportunities to scale up probabilities of eradicating impossibilities. The teacher of our problems are problems lying in the path.

<u>Bring Positive Attitude Towards Human Beings</u>

Family members make our day, society binds, helps us to enjoy our moment. Success is multiplied when shared, happiness yields from the feedbacks of your loved ones. Its all about human. Human beings are creatures which help someone to blossom and of course all of us have an attitude towards human.

Human beings, people makes us live. It is the people who make us succeed. Successful people will always have positive thought process towards people. If I want success I should make it happen that my people will make it better than I perceive. We need help to get something worth. We walk after birth, holding hands of parents, and later in life god will make sure that someone comes and catch hold of our hand towards the destination of success. The positive attitude towards human beings will always help us find God beside us to walk the path. He is always with us, the source of abundance manifests its presence always. The attitude, gratitude will help us feel God is with us. It is nothing but how we see human beings.

We hinder this feeling with EGO—"Edging God Out". This compel people think of all accomplishment is by virtue of his talent, hard work etc...etc.. This is nothing but lack of Gratitude towards source which has always been with us wherever we are. This ego inhibits people to turn around the success in multifold. Power thinkers believe that people will trust him, believe in his ideas, and accept his wisdom and advice. They always contemplate contribution of people towards their success and happiness. There are people have none at their funeral but only have God beside to make him free from this universe. It is the people who make you reckon or make you lonely.

People make us, love brings us love, hatred brings us hatred. It is just a law of attraction. Being Good is only way to serve God. Good will only manifest God. Good is all about being fabulous in all approach, starting from thinking Good to doing Good. You are serving god and God will always be beside you. Emotions makes you closer to people and being good to people.

Here we need to inspire others. Inspiring others is also respecting their ideas, their thought process. Idea is all actually coming from our source who has only one agenda, which is betterment of us. Inspiring others is all only keeping faith in God.

Idea only brings change in life. Someone will be inspired only if we understand his need and his personal and professional belief. To make someone inspired he has to be nurtured firstly with a great deal of faith.

<u>Thinking Positive about Your Emotions</u>

Energetic thinkers think possible. They generate a feeling of worth which creates emotions which actually attracts great things happening. Just think opposite, thinking impossible will create an emotion of sorrow, grief. Replacing negative emotions with positive emotions will only make us energetic thinker.

Negative emotions can also be constructive, provided they are intended well. Good Intention will only bring back good result. But the crux of the matter is how we control the emotion to make us better human being. Be happy attitude always, irrespective of unhappiness around, we will feel possibility in returning and we be happy. Energetic thinkers can always remember the good moments of their life. However bad phases have come, but remembering good phases replace good. It is only God makes good and hence worship happens.

In our life we assume that we are meant for something or asked to do something which is not generally of our kind, we don't want to do that. But we do it forcibly. We do it and think, alas! we never had gone into, but we couldn't avoid!! It makes us take a backseat and always being apprehensive. But if we do it with clear heart it may make us learn so many good things. We thought badly because of our limited thought, belief or imaginations. But rather being unhappy, and cursing one, just thinking whatever has been happening is happening for good, will help us replace bad thoughts with good one. We have heroes who has come out of all odds with these thought process only. When India wanted freedom, all violent resistant had been converted into non violent and India got their cherished freedom back. It is nothing but belief of your good thought and control over emotions.

"Never let a problem become your excuse"

World class life, everyone's dream. Ideas will come play a vital role. We are born, a child under influence of parents. Parents try to tell us good things to follow, good things to see, good things to do. Children are great learner. As we know childhood brings us all learning. Crafting a world class life starts from childhood. We see things, try to imitate during childhood, without understanding what would be its implication, good implications or bad results. We are creative when child. Abundance of new ideas flows freely. Children do not have prejudice, they do not have burden of experience which actually hinders idea to flow. But the question is being adult, do we encourage their ideas always which children bring to us! No, and certainly our beliefs stops us encouraging them. We keep on thinking what to do, we keep on guessing the implications, which propel us to go back and say "not a right idea" and shatter the hopes of those. We say to them, they should not do this rather they should think like this, which is nothing but generated from our beliefs. We, the elders, see the world through a tainted glass of our experience, belief, understandings. The moment we stop children to execute their creativity, we unknowingly has given them a massage of all our beliefs, which is a life of all about set rules, which we should follow. They are told to behave likewise. If children are allowed to think freely, that will help their life to bring in excellent results and will of course help them to build a world class life. Why the adults don't understand, if all of us doing right things we would have crafted a different life, not a life of mediocrity. People spend their years with the same office, same breakfast, same set of rules. A child cries to get the things done in favour of them, but as they grow up they leave that, since they are repeatedly told it is not the righ way, it should not be like this, it is the good way etc etc and the adolescents or youth learn to live life which is nothing but some set rules. They always fail to achieve though those set rules and condemn their luck, destiny and so on.......................... The failure of channelizing our energy in a right direction when grown up is nothing but we never learnt how to do that during childhood. You see a child, you see his behavior, they grasp things faster. We just need to inculcate a sense of belief in the child that the ideas are worth considering and they should live them.

Youth, abundance of energy. They go on achieveing those recognitions which gives the young generation a feel of completeness. They think of goals but can only achieve them if they are able to channelize energy in the right direction. The energy of thought, self reliance will only help them create huge positive energy. Being a self believer only happens during this tenure of life, the key here is self reliance. This is the power which actually helps them eradicating negative thoughts. Good energy will only help them manifesting good and will help eliminating worst. Young generation to be told to believe their ideas, to be told to respect their ideas of life which will help them to craft a world class life. Human beings, believes in seeing, believes in tangible existence of things and then able to visualize the thought. Thought come from idea will only can shape good. We see things happening. That's how we refer something to establish benchmark and go towards this. We relate to reference points:

My Mother—Reference point of kindness

My Father—reference point of disciplined life

Mahatma Gandhi—reference point of self believer

Nelson Mandlea: Reference point of courage

Youth, when crafting his life through execution of ideas will easily relate to those reference points, we only need to tell them, direct them to follow their ideas, their dreams. All great people achieved their destiny by thinking differently. Youths, if start thinking by breaking the bonds of rules will only manifest their dream come true.

Crafting a world class life or follow a dream is only about thinking differently. Firm believer of ideas, can see problems as milestones of learning, can encourage failure to go ahead and achieve a world class life. A seed of idea if nurtured, may create wonders in every phase of life.

Keeping positive about your emotions will also demand keeping positive about others as well. The seed of trust for others will make others believe you. Positive attitude towards others will also will help develop the trust.

The trust, to make it happen we need to follow some important steps. Those we will see in our next chapters.

Ideas and its essence:

Ideas will flow, when you ASPIRE. Affirming some action will help you aspire. Your idea of getting good job, affirming right steps and continuous perseverance will help you aspire. You can learn to achieve, you can succeed, but only you need to aspire. Everyone has privilege to deserve success. It is not that successful people are more blessed than you, but they aspires differently.

1. GOD HELPS THOSE WHO HELP THEMSELVES.

Beginning is half done…. BEGIN to dream, begin to believe, and begin to behold faith. Aspiration will only turn to be true when you begin to execute. Knowing is not all about without doing. Doing will only fulfill knowing. You can fulfill your aspiration somewhere in future, which will not necessarily be the same place as you are here today. It is the beginning of something somewhere, which helps you to fulfill and to aspire, to achieve and to make your dream fulfilled. Develop courage, conviction of getting greatness will only drive us to manifest result. Follow and do all those small things with courage and conviction. It is only energy which exists and the same energy will help things shape up. When we are inspired with a dream God has given us a ball to play as dream, but courage will help us hit the ball and start playing. Most people forget to develop courage and follow it life through.

DREAM to make your life extraordinary. Caring dream and pursue all across life is the essence of life. Ordinary people with mediocrity do not dare to dream. A seed of idea will generate dream will in turn change the life.

EMPOWER yourself through education. Education brings us knowledge and knowledge brings us empowerment. It helps determine the path, since education determines awareness which determines choice and choice determines result. Result brings us empowerment. Idea of being empowered, follow the right path helps us achieve our destiny. Feeling empowered by all thoughts will be the strength. Empowerment is a flow of energy which further helps us achieve. Empowerment is the MANTRA of achievement.

FETCH the result. Predicting result and finding the treasure of success. Success is always concealed as Diamonds are in deep in the mine. It is the God who does not put up treasures in the open; he always conceals the matter, because something which is achieved fetched into existence is more valuable. We become EnergeticThinker, we have all possibilities within ourselves. We have hidden treasures within us, a seed of idea will fetch that treasure out. We underestimate the treasure and as we grow up we tend to separate ourselves from finding the same and with all possibilities we live mediocrity.

GOING TO GIVE:

This is the attitude of ensuring return exponentially. The thought to give, share increases hidden treasure within us. A man, who thinks of giving all his talent for the betterment of the company, will always add value which is more than its paycheck. We have five stages in life, Nesting, Testing, Investing, Arresting and cresting phase. The investing phase is the phase where in we invest all we have as treasure to bring in more treasure. The risk of life lies here and giving gets us the door open of next possibilities.

NO REJECTION:

"I find hope in the darkest of days and focus in the brightest. I do not judge the universe"—Dalai Lama

Never reject an idea, because reasoning of rejection is our limitations, which we need to transcend. 'Because it is wrong'… we with our limitations easily reject an idea thinking that it is wrong. It is astonishing that people gather together and find fault in an opportunity. It is very easy to throw a problem, but taking away negative will only get us positive. Every idea has enormous positivity, but our job is to find it out. If I tell you, I am writing a book, I only had an idea, but no where I could see it or even I could feel that I could do this, but today it is in front of you.

2. NOT SURE OF SUCCESS, IDEA SHOULD NOT BE DUMPED:

Ego, a state of mind which is always keeping yourself with a high materialistic esteem, in turn makes you away from God. Dr. Dyer said EGO is Edging God Out. Our awareness of success creates ego and we come out from being humble. Idea, which is a massage of God edged out automatically.

a. Because of Non adaptability of Change:

Customisation, adjustments, compromise, sacrifice, accommodation of changes is the essence. Getting these into daily practice is not easy and idea, a massage from God, should not be rejected because we are not able to adjust, or else we are not able to accommodate changes. Every tension brings in opportunity in abundance but exploring opportunity is idea exploration.

b.   Because of conflict:

Energetic thinking will only give us a lesson, that problem will only result possibility. A goal will only be achieved through crossing a set of hurdles. Conflicts will come in our way of success, because of different thought process which is generated.

c.   Because of Non Availability of resource:

The best example is to quote here is every day's idea at our workplace, gets rejected because, scarcity of resource, in terms of money, machine etc. But thinking differently and optimum utilization of resource only makes someone rockstar at work. Hence non availibilty of manpower, money etc one should not reject an idea. It is all about strategy. When strategy is multiplied with resource, results manifest. This is only being done through infinite intelligence, accumulated Experience, Experiment and research. But ideas can be impemented through a master mind.

d.   Because we do not get credit:

We never appreciate our parents for their deeds, but we always think it is their responsibility. Aspiring to get due credit of our ideas will diminish our energetic thinking abilities, it is sure that God has kept something more to get credit. Decisions should never be based on ego needs, but it should be based on accomplishing the need to fulfill goal.

"If you always do what you always did, you will always get what you always got"

Points of IDEA---which makes us dream.

1.   Ideas if nurtured make us Energetic Thinker.

2. Be aware of:

    a. Bringing Positive attitude
    b. Attaining self leadership
    c. Bringing positive attitude towards changes
    d. Bringing Positive Attitude towards Human Beings
    e. Being positive about own Emothions.

3. Do the Followings

    a. Dream to make life extraordinary
    b. Empower yourself through education
    c. Fetch the result
    d. Going to give
    e. No Rejection.

Chapter 2

FAITH: INDUCED BY AUTO SUGGESTION

Thoughts, seeds of our belief system, only produce faith. Faith within you will only bring in a successful individual.

"There are people in the world so hungry, that God can not appear to them, except in the form of Bread"---Mahatma Gandhi

Life gives us all in abundance. Universe has created all in plenty. If every single individual has a faith of achieving in life he/she wants to manifest, universe will give him /her multiples in return. Key to get it is our faith.

We fail to believe, we fail to think, we fail to execute. The feeling of failure is so huge; we never come out of it. But opposite side of the coin is, we succeed we are fulfilled, we receive all glory. Its also huge that one goes on achieving. Scientists in search of something, uses all experiments, theory, refers all past achievements—but the crux is "Faith" of searching which is never seen.

"To believe in the things you can see and touch is no belief at all: but to believe in the unseen is a triumph and blessing"- Abraham Lincoln

Your beliefs are from your own world. It may be true or untrue. But what true you imagine it becomes truth of your life. Since all you are attracting towards you its true to the universe. May be bad or good to you, but universe can not sense it, since it is law of attraction.

The reality of you are being unlimited. There are huge possibilities which we can not see but all are prevailing. What we need to do is to start thinking of amazing successful life.

Faith in Love, all good things in this world can be achieved through love only. You love yourself to love others. You show love get love in return. All possibilities are love centric only. Give love as much as you can, the force of love will surround you with good people, circumstances and opportunities. Believe in whatever you want you will get. Whatever you want to be you will be.

Once I was discussing potential of my elder daughter with her only sitting during one Sunday dinner. She has been pretty good in singing and of course in dancing. She used to learn Classical Indian Dance long back and also used to win various prizes in different Dance competitions. But she left dancing and also left showing interest in that too. Also she used to score marks in School Exams and her teachers always had been praising. Also she was not very keen to maintain her study as well. We were just discussing what makes her good. I told about her ability to showcase her talents which are phenomenal, and fortunately she accepted that fact, it is only her will which makes her perform, whatever she wants to. I was never trying to rebuke her, for not taking things seriously or for not exploring her natural talents exposed and sharpened. I was only trying to ask her the reasons of non participation. She was silent, not able to answer me, but she did also not know the reasons. She only could make me understand that she just does not like those now. I only told her one thing, if you have faith in you no matter how much you waste time, you will always be praised. She was surprised by my words, she was actually waiting for some words of reprimand from me then. I was very much sure of her inheritance. I told her, you do small but try to do it for yourself and of course for your inner satisfaction. I have that trust in you that you will surely bring in result with effort, but the result will only come when you have faith in you. I assured her about my faith to her. After that she had been only doing things which makes her feel good, even if she understood she has that talent but only faith in her, love in her will bring in all positive outcomes. My younger daughter has tremendous faith in herself, which is making her confident which I am proud of.

I only helped her to make her believe herself. I only tried to develop faith in her. I also know the faith of mine has only been manifested to make her believing herself. Here it is all about fetching the result you want to be manifested. It starts from you not from an outside world. Your failth, your own belief will bring in positive influence to others life that you love.

Thoughts and Faith:

We have huge number of thoughts everyday. Thoughts drive us. In this universe our thoughts only attracts the happenings. It is the law of attraction. Human beings believe in seen and build their dream on it. Rarest of the people think of unseen, have belief and run behind to achive that. That is faith, which has been continuously generated from our thoughts.

Faith is Power. It never fails. A person having faith to succeed will always succeed, but occassionaly faith never make us give up, we give up faith and get away from the path to succeed. The power of faith only comes when we control our thought process. Thinking only will create a field of energy. Faith comes from the thought. Positive thought helps building strong faith. Faith in yourself, is the faith towards abundance of universe. Faith is only like formation of plant. First plant the seed, spray water to sprout. Once sprouted then only fruit will come and we would be able to see result.

The current reality of us or our current life is the result of thought you have been thinking. The book which I am writng had become a thought a few years before now it's a reality. What has happened?? It is nothing, the thought which changed the feeling.

We have good and bad thoughts simultaneously. We as human being always tend to indulge into bad thoughts and we experience its multiplication which simply just resembles with Embryo and slowly it becomes our feeling which is BAD.

Positive thoughts, has to be nurtured. These thoughts only will create positive feelings and these feelings will bring in faith. Positive faith will only bring positive change to our lives.

How to DEMAND:

Our thoughts will only make us demand what we want to be, we want to be rich, with all materialistic possession, have a picture in your mind what you would like to have when you have abundance of money. You think of having all luxuries which you think you should posses that day. But demand of you being rich will get you there.

Also we need to understand how learning will change our life. How will we understand learning to demand has actually manifested. It simply manifested, you will surely have all desires as demanded.

Understand what you demand. How consistently you can demand. How faithfully you can demand. There are some deposits to make things happen in your life. Those deposits will only bring in positive results.

Understand your Demand: It is only to understand what you need to sacrifice to make demand consistent and which is with immense faith. You need to sacrifice your instability of thought, your habit of being reactive with result.

Keep Promises to yourself: Keep always promises to yourself. Your demand is only to keep those strong faith intact. You sacrifice mood.

Being Honest with yourself: You sacrifice ego, arrogance. You can only demand by being true with you, honest with you.

How to have DESIRE:

You should believe that you have received what richness you are supposed to have. You must pretend, visualize the richness and materialistic belongings you expect you posses when you become rich. Desire gives you all what you would like to receive.

Desiring is aspiring, motivating ourselves towards certain goal or achievements. Demand a desire. We believe in seen but what we have seen we can have desires. No one of us has low potential or strength to reach the point of his desire, it just to keep your aspiration intact. You see them regularly happening in your life, you see them present in your life, you manifest them in your feeling of pleasure. NO rule what to desire, no specifications of desire, but be clear about what you want something to get manifested in your life.

You may observe, things are not moving right as desired. Look back at you. Understand one thing, it is of course relative. It starts from you and ends at you. You may have failed to get those feeling inside or you couldn't follow them continuously since life has so many daily challenges, which debars us manifesting our desires. We then blame our luck, which is only brought by you through visualizing your desire.

How to RECEIVE:

Feel good, you should always feel good. Receive all happenings with same enthusiasm and see it will gain multiples. The concentration and being focused about the positive feelings of receiving will only make this happen. Time of receipt also depends on your thought. Composed thought, conviction in thinking will reduce or increase timeline to receive it.

Here we need to learn what make us keep the thought process of gratitude while receiving our desire. Simultaneously we need to take care of followings:

Enthusiasm: It is all about excitement. The feeling of good. But are you able to get excited or remain energetic always! No, we get sorrow when we receive defeat, when we receive demotivating results. Learn to be enthusiastic then; this may sound ridiculous, but this is true, this will only manifest result.

Once I started a business of establishing an Institution of training for Hotel people. Three friend of us started a joint venture and was actually thought of putting all of our effort to make it a success. We started collecting money, and slowly took a place on rent and purchased all necessary things to get that Institutes started. We hired people to run that place. We always had in mind, students or prospective candidates who will take admission will only make this place running. We did all possible effort to get students admitted. But it was a total failure. We could not make it. Disappointment, family anguish and all related negatives started prevailing around all of us. When today it is analyzed, we find we missed in establishing "why" we wanted to make it. Rather we did all "what" to make that run. We never got enthusiastic with the learnings of failure. But I did one thing, I thought of getting out of my comfort zone first to clear my debts and then after to learn what potential I have. I got out of my comfort zone, left the secured job and joined somewhere. Today if I go back and see, the excitement of repaying the debt and knowing self made this happen and today I am dreaming to destine.

Positive feeling about receiving:

Very essential attribute of receiving. Positive feeling will only make this happen. We received good, don't we think it would have been much better!!! We received bad, don't we think its all because of external influence and our luck never favored!!

Here we need to learn to emanate positivity while we receive both good or bad. When we receive good, gratitude and being thankful of whatever we received, will surely multiply the receipt. Hence thinking of what not received will not help us receive more. It always happens with us when we get some rewards or incentive or appreciation for some good job. We think it would have been much better if we would have done this. But we seldom forget to maintain our positive energy for longer period of time for the receipt of achievement. We loose focus of being positive and start spending time on non receipt. Hence we never attract larger achievements in future. Learning to be good, feel great with even smaller achievement will bring in bigger achievements.

Keeping eye or control on time: It is all about when we want things to happen. It does also depend on us. It is how we want things to get manifested in our life. I wanted to travel by air and always in a car when I was serving a Government organization. But I always thought about travelling on that mode. But never used to know how would that be possible.

But today I only travel in that mode only. It is just within 10 years everything got changed. I feel excited about it, but also think I would have controlled the time also and would have got that long before, if I could believe in me.

Its all within us, the way you think you generate faith and get rewarded with all demands and desires.

Faith with Change:

Change is the truth of life. Our body cells are almost replaced within every few months. We as human being change within, but we can never feel it, but it is only energy which help us change. Faith in change is the faith towards universe.

Adaptibility or being adaptable is the essence of seeing and getting good result from faith. Faith in you can move mountains. When we want to change our circumstances, we must change our thinking. The change which is happening to us everyday, we only get them attracted in our life.

"when you are through changing, you are through"

How to Trust:

Trust in you will help other trust you. Trust in you, it just not happen, it is to be believed. Faith of trust will bring in trust within.

Building Faith:

All of us think, if we build faith, then only things start coming in. But building faith and continuously following to attain desire, where we fail occasionally. The method of building faith is very difficult to describe, but if you feel it's very easy to see. It's only an inside out approach. Our limbic brain gives us trust, faith and love, which are getting out through our language. Building faith is only intellect which we may think as waste. It is to develop peace within you and the peace, serenity and feel of peace will only help us build faith. Heart creates our Emotional intelligence which is enabling us to make this possible.

The subconscious mind plays an important role in developing faith. Subconscious mind only understands repetition and affirmation of desires and we develop faith. Repetitive thoughts which passes through our subconscious mind becomes faith and manifestation become happening. What we think inside manifests outside. Faith is the initiation of all result. Faith is the ways and means to bring in abundance.

Your conviction and faith:

Our abilities, drives us. Knowing our abilities, seems to be tough. But desire will fetch in abilities to accomplish.

The dominating thoughts will automatically bring in the change which is desired. Accomplishment will only come by regular pursuation. Practicing daily, the habit of persistent thought which drives to the attainment of desire, only will bring conviction. Continuous elimination of negative situations of environment and from within will help go forward and we achieve destiny.

Conviction, driving and making happen is continuous practice. It emanates with strong will power. Will power is only self driven. You will only enhance, increase or reduce, diminish will power. Yes will power and conviction has a relationship and it is through stroke. Positive stroke of good job. At different phases of life conviction level changes which is dependent on various experiences.

Childhood; Learning Phase of our life. We study, go to school and learn basics of life. The same learning is being measured by results of our Examinations. Conviction towards learning varies from kid to kid. We have seen too much persuasive parents who compels their child to study always make it monotonous for them. We also have seen kids do not study at all. We also have seen kids does good without even touching the books. The common in all these here is not different learning abilities, the common here is how they are enjoying study. Parents should make it enjoyable and playful. Enjoyable and playful atmosphere will help them learn more, since kids will add their enormous creativity to understand the subject much better. Here, in childhood, providing the playful atmosphere will only bring their conviction out to study and learn.

We get into youth and slowly into adult phase and conviction of adapting change in life is important here. Here in we need strokes towards acknowledging good job. The result of positive feedback will be multiple times more than criticism. We can easily enhance motivation of someone through patting on back and making him doing the job more efficiently and effectively. Conviction comes with motivation and motivation comes from encouragement and positive feedback.

Source, intention and Faith:

The source we come from is an energy field. The source is only our identity. A piece of apple if separated out and claimed to have separate identity, then it is simply ignoring its source from where it has originated. We live, we spend days, and our ego of self achievement makes us away from the source we originated. We fail to establish a link with our source. Our ego, self non awareness makes this link feeble, almost nonexistent. All of us are driven by the source from which all of us emanate. But our achievements, our sorrow, our experience makes us forget about that abundance which universe has already offered us. Abundance of everything, this universe has been creating this abundance every time. You think of receiving it, you receive. Connecting to the source and believing you are driven by faith. The same faith will allow you get connected with your source.

Faith brings in attitude. Here to quote about Mr. Sachin Tendulkar—who had talent, had all spark of being genius. But above all his faith made him believe about his abilities. When he could play more than 50 matches without taking rest for single day, which is surely an outcome of his huge huge faith. The faith only manifested talent within him. Scientists search for unseen, unheard and unknown. They invent, but the courage of invention is only faith. They go beyond, think differently and search for something new. They connect with source, extreme faith in the universe makes them invent and civilization gets benefitted.

Magic of Faith:

We create our own world. If we see outside through a rough glass we see an unclear world but if the glass is clear we see a clear world. It is only in seeing with your eyes which has faith of seeing clear things. We only create the appearance of the world. It is no one which can make you unstable, unfulfilling, and unhappy other than you.

"State of mind must be belief, not hope or wish". Your challenge will only be solved by you. We think God will come and resolve our problem. When we overcome, we think and realize God has helped us with all ideas, but execution lies with us. Faith of the Idea lies with us. We only make us unstable by not using our faith.

"Every adversity brings with it, the seed of equivalent advantage"

Faith brings in abundance. But the magic is creating faith and believing it. We plant a seed, we expect it will grow and give us fruit one day. The faith of getting the fruit is the magic and that will fetch us fruit one day. It is same in all aspect of life. We harvest, we sprinkle water to the tree, we provide all suitable atmosphere which will help it grow and it grows. The water of our life is gratitude. Gratitude helps us grow and nurtures our attitude towards every single creature of universe, which is making our life living everyday, is the key go big.

Faith works magically on us. It will create fruit for us in abundance. You believe in being rich, being successful....but the point here is show gratitude first to the thought of getting rich and successful.

Visualization of your attainment, only fetch all in reality. The desire list, which all of us have will only get manifested when we actually feel it. Saying thank you, showing gratitude towards attainment of that desire will only help that fetch into our life. Say thank you to the air, oxygen, sunlight, roads...etc which we see, use every day to live happily. The more you say thank you the more you receive. Gratitude is only key which makes our life full of abundance. God has given us everything, he is just waiting for the gratitude we share.

"It is easier for God to say no to us, than for him to get us to say YES to him."

Points of Faith: Enlightening your Dream-

Let us summarize all points of faith. This is the only key to reach to your dream.

a. Thoughts energize your faith.
b. Have faith in change
c. Build faith with a process of thoughts
d. Relate conviction with faith
e. Have faith in your source or intention

Chapter 3

EMERGE LIFE WITH DREAMING

We dream in every stage of life by knowing or not knowing it. Dream prevails in every stages of life. We start dreaming from childhood.

Our birth gifts; everyone comes in this world with these gifts which are common for every human being. But life, society and so called rules to live, make us forget about the birth gifts. God has given all of us equal possessions. The problem of not using our birth gifts is only non awareness about them. Again to reiterate, awareness precedes choice and choices precede result.

We start dreaming from childhood. We feel secured always in childhood. We can think, adopt and practice anything without any prejudice, without any contemplation. We are free to choose during childhood. Free to act, free to communicate, free to dream. All we do during our childhood is the manifestation of reference points.

Reference points, to understand it better, we follow someone or imitate someone during our life. We follow the reference points. We believe what we see, what is happening around without any prejudice. It is moreover seeing and following. We see things or we see others doing it. At first we start believing that.

In my own life I have faced days of not being decisive and only attracted tension, agony. It is one of the characteristic of human being, to refer something which is already practiced. It is mostly seen, human get perplexed by choosing common paths.

We refer to all existing happenings of the world. We refer to intelligent class mates during our school days; we refer their scores in exam, their stories of intelligence and think that it can be achievable. When we understand or see our reference points are achieving, we start striving to achieve this. Our parents

Rupak Aich

quote those examples of achievements. I used to secure good marks and used to secure good ranks in the class. During my class 7th in Kolkata, I slipped to rank to 3rd and I faced sarcasm of my aunty and got scolded throughout the day. She had been very critical analyzing the facilities we used to get compared to facilities my aunty used to get during their school days, which happened to be better during our day. Her main point was, in spite of all worthy support from our parent I was not capable of make them proud of me. I was upset and never wanted to show my face to my parents. Then I started thinking about 1st ranker of my class and kept on referring him. Wanted to understand what he did extra to become 1st Ranker in the class. Hence I started referring him and he became my source of inspiration and my reference point. It was easy to understand the gaps of efforts I put across for study. Referring a reference point will always help you stretch and do those extras which bring result. Then only you start transcending limitations and all dormant forces come into play to bring you up.

We reach our dream only by following certain steps which are already taken by our reference points. We just need to follow them.

Childhood and reference points:

Children are always free from all prejudice which an adult will always have. Children do things which they always like. They do not bother for implications, result of whatever they do. They do things with lots of innovation, since they can think better. They think freely and being unaware of result. It is all about their good feeling. They do not know social, mental so called ethics. When we were child we thought of becoming beaurocrat, poet, and journalist....so many. Slowly we get out of those when got adult and got influenced by speed of life rather influencing life. We could think dream, desire, more effectively during childhood. No negative thoughts used to crop up.

Children always imitate. They imitate cartoon characters, they imitate heros, they imitate their elders, their parents. They always with their natural thinking abilities will try and follow those. They will always behave in the same way as their referenece points would be. At school, they are being told about social heros, their sacrifices etc. We only do it to help them learn good things. They have been always taught to be good and follow good.

They have all abilities to choose good because they understand feelings. They believe in their belief which is faith. We should make them do what ever they wanted to do. But now the question is after they are exposed to so many reference points, why they fail sometime? We, elders, parents, always see things as we are thinking. We always tell them to do good but often fail to demonstrate the same. But when we see world, our societal system, we compel children to do what fits the society. We always forget about their natural thinking abilities. If you want to make your child a hero, behave like a hero, think differently and show them your faith to them and to the world of abundance. Children refer their parents. If parents fail to behave as ideal reference point then all education fails.

Developing faith in them about themselves is important. To make them dream. We often see, during childhood we can dream to have the greatest success in the world, but these dreams dissolves as we grow up. We are then controlled by thoughts which are developed with days passed by. We forget our all childhood dreams and slowly turn into a character that does not have any dream, or we never dare to dream when we grow up.

All of us think and feel, childhood days are best days in life, but when we grow up why can't we see our days differently. Why can't we think or why do we lose faith in self? Why do we forget that our days are created by us, no one else. We neglect our ideas. But during childhood we never thought like that. It does not mean that the reasons were not there, but as a child we never used to get perturbed. Hence getting confused, being perturbed and stop dreaming is only in our hand, we can only create our life.

The difference of thought has been always influencing our future. The thought difference of childhood and later; influences our destiny. We should have faith in our ideas which is only of us. These should be free from any influence. Key of success is you think that you can do everything which you dream. We all have all talents which are required to be great, to be successful. Being playful when we are adult is seldom seen.; being free in thoughts, allowing dormant forces to work for you, transcending your limitations make us great, make us dream.

"A man is the product of his thoughts, what he thinks he can become"--- Mahatma Gandhi.

<u>Believe in yourself when you are young:</u>

Crossing teens and getting into youth is only about changing or developing priorities of life. But we should focus. Faith and belief takes a back seat when we see regular life happenings. This is the time when we should clearly understand our goal. We should clearly make a path of destiny. With abundant energy and vitality the faith in self drives all activities.

It is very easy to get carried away or very easy to become non focused. The daily referring points makes us belief, why not...why not. Faith plays an important role in that. Faith in self, and definite belief of achieving only will help us choose our way forward. Dreams drive strongly when we are young and I think it is the strongest when we follow that. It is always preferable to a have a GURU, when we are young; to guide us overcome daily obstacles and help we find our way.

"An error does not become truth by reason of multiplied propagation, nor does truth becomes error, because nobody sees it"—Mahatma Gandhi

Youth has all energy but the requirement is only to put all those towards right direction. Negative thoughts are like embrio, it grows in multiples. Non achievements of any kind obstruct or rather misdirect youths. They get into negative thought process. This is the phase of life when we get to have experiences. The real life, its experience changes in our daily life. But if we know our destiny, if we believe in ourselves, we will surely get there where we dream to be.

Here is the time to recognize the abundance of universe. Here is the time when we should belief that we are one part of the Source. We have a role to play. Distractions need to be utilized in a positive way; it should only be looked into a better way to get into the right track. But our dreams have to be very clear. Practicing those thought process will only attract all resources to fulfill it. The feeling of achievements will create your destiny. Learn how to dream, learn how to have desires in life, see them happening and automatically it will manifest.

"I find the hopes in darkest of days, and focus in the brightest. I do not judge the universe"---Dalai Lama

Youth is all about creating, youth is all about making. Hence create a life which is full of desires.

"In order to carry a positive active action we must develop here a positive vision"---Dalai Lama

Belief in yourself when adult:

We say, we are done, we say nothing more to achieve, since we think that we have no luck. We also think we don't have sufficient skill set to achieve dreams which were always a part of us during childhood or youth. We say, change can only happen to other not to self. It is all about self image. You chose to be mediocre because our surroundings say so. We are happy with same routine since last 10 years, happy with same work since last 10 years, happy with same breakfast since last 10 years. If we don't look at changing our daily routine, it never changes. As an example if we go out from home to a trip somewhere, our whole routine gets disturbed but we can still be alive and working. It is all about seeing change and adapting it. No one will come or approach you from outside to make changes in your life. It is me who is going to change the whole world around me. Heroes see things differently. They do things differently, they do right things but not popular things.

We talked of faith in our last chapter. We mentioned, belief only brings faith in us. Growing up or being adult does not mean that we have lost time of building faith in us again. Failure is never final. We may have failed in various other affairs, but should we remember those failures and believe that I can't do it. Failure and success are all same, only difference is to feel it. It is more than winning or losing. Winners if can't improve themselves regularly will surely encounter failure. The success is accepting the opportunities and giving your best. An athlete's effort is never complete or nor does he wins until he fails to break previous record. It is just discovering your inner potential and abilities to see new opportunities.

We see never ending problems in our daily life. One success brings in problems as well. You step into a ladder of success, a new sets of challenge will suddenly appear. Hence getting perturbed and obtaining monotony, lethargy by these challenges is the reason of failure. Success will finally be understood by measuring how graceful, happy, polite, positive you are during this process. Believing in you throughout this whole process is real success. You are able to make it, you are then able to reach destination, and you are then able to have prosperity. The spark within you is now come out; the ignition is only your belief.

You make your life. You only can fulfill the dream. You are only responsible. You need to start, hold and fulfill. Everything starts at you, ends at you.

"Courage is something you can never lose. Because courage is something which you can always choose."

Chapter 4

INFLUENCE YOURSELF

You think of mastery, you create it. You think of elegance you create it. You think of specialty you create if. Nothing in this world can make you stop, if you don't want to be stopped. Try Influencing others, do manifestation of some good habits, try influencing self and also know yourself.

Everyone in this world knows his or her outer world. But knowing you….. "Who am I" is a question in every one's mind. Heroes are asked how they have achieved this destination. But I have seen every hero speaks the same, they say you know yourself, believe in yourself, you get it. Is this sentence is that simple as it is seen or spelt? Know Yourself----what does it mean???? Every human being claims a name, an identity, speaks about his qualification, his material belongings, about his possessions. As per law, every orderly thing will become disorderly with course of time. Hence the belongings will also perish. Perishability comes with every materialistic belonging.

But the question remains same---"who am I".

The world is crated with all natural resources which is required for life to live. Life and being lively is a continuous process. But the worldly resources which make life never reduced by volume or quantity. But gratitude towards same is seldom found in human being. Gratitude is the key to get everything in abundance. What is luck, is it a destiny or is it a choice? Destiny and choice make us think….. We already know choice precedes result. Hence if we can see luck as a choice it shall yield result.

To understand choice, let us understand our birth gifts. Birth gifts are equal and abundant for every human being. The first birth gift is "CHOICE"… freedom to choose. Simply put together, stimulus creates response. But we have choice of response. We can choose response. This varies individual to individual; few persons don't choose, only responds and think its pros and cons. Some choose, think and respond, it surely yield better result. The gap between stimuli and the liberty of choice lies in varies from individual to individual. But liberty to choose is with every human being since birth. To phrase it in a better way we can say, choice lies with you, you choose and respond. Hence choosing gratitude is your wish, more you are thankful more you get.

"Freedom to Choose" is actually first step which help you influencing yourself. Very easy to say, follow safety norms, everywhere it is written STOPLOOK-GO. I think that's my choice... to Look... be Safe and Go. Being safe is your choice. You choose and be happy. More we practice to have choices more options we have. But the question is how we can improve the gap between stimulus and response. i.e. how will we learn to have more choices. It is nothing but awareness...

Describing awareness is not the intention here, but the intention is how to be aware? We have books, we have biographies. we have mentors, we have Gurus, we have friends, we have God always, this list is endless. But believe in the source from where we have come, the source will make you aware if you trust in him. God is everywhere, always helping us. Seek his help to become aware. The feeling of God making us aware is beyond any expressions. Being aware, believing it and practicing it, will only help us realize how efficient we are for choices.

Choice, choosing for self, we think how I can influence my choice. We should start thinking of the sources of our learning .... our societal rules, talks of our elders, responsibilities of our surroundings, duty towards family etc etc. Hence we do what the whole world do generally, no other approach; simply we follow customs and practices. This is mediocrity. Very easy to take that approach, we satisfy ourselves thinking that, I have made other person happy where in I am not.... But the question is, if I am not happy or positive I cannot bring happiness or positivity in my life, I can't make others happy. Hence the choice we make based on our mediocre learning does not help. Therefore, learn to choose. It will only help you fight odds. The right choice will keep you happy and your actions will be in sync with this.

Predicting result is actually choosing right. The message, ideas, faith, trusts, whatever we speak is all about how you make your choices and how do you predict result. Predicting result is only influenced by choice. You choose and get result. Establishing right result is nothing but choosing right.

We know natural laws, which are not changeable since the principles of law cannot change. Time is powerful. Time controls everything, we the human beings cannot influence cycle of time. The strength of time is a truth and similarly with all natural laws as well. All laws are applicable to all of us since birth. These laws influence us and we get influenced. Principles like kindness, softness, trust, faithfulness etc. are not changeable or even negotiable. Kindness is a principle which is to be understood in true sense. Hence all "Natural laws influence us".

"Natural laws influence us".

But we need to understand how they influence us. Getting into terrace of a building and jumping down, will nowhere bring him upward, he will only move downward because of gravitation. Hence choosing to jump is how you influence yourself. Gratitude, Kindness, Forgiveness are non negotiable. Principles influence us, and the influence makes us act. The act of kindness will always bring in kindness; the act of forgiveness will actually make you free from all mental burdens. Stress, Agony, Tension are not principles. They are made by us. We forget to be kind, we forget to be faithful, we forget to be loved and we produce tension, stress in our life. As soon as we create the atmosphere of negative energy around us, the negative energy enters in our life. We tend be in grief, greater sorrow and sometime it becomes unbearable. The understanding here is ignoring principles of positive energy and hence influenced.

Again we do not know us or we do not want to be different. Being different is just thinking different. The energy in us, the strength in us, is immense, since our sprit is immortal. It never dies. Piece, Love in abundance is the characteristic of spirit. Body is only the temple of that energy. Spirit is love, spirit is kind, spirit is everything. As soon as we identity our self an energy field of huge potential, we connect to our source. All science has understood the energy within which can only be felt.

Principles and natural law help our spirit attract strength and we make our lives beautiful.

All stimuli does not work identically with all people. A common stimulus can be different for every individual. A movie make with a Story line, gives different stimuli to different people. Hence choice to respond every human being have. The choice of being reactive, proactive, is only with you.

Knowing Intelligences: Towards influencing yourself

We all have intelligence…. "Intelligences" is another factor which is with us since birth. Understanding intelligence and moreover being passionate about it is what we miss in our life. Mind, Body, Soul and Heart, create our intelligences.

Souls, regulates body, regulates power…… calmness, loveful, peaceful and powerful are only truth. Knowing me is not the name, profession, religion, relation… these are all mine, but who am I. I am energy of Love, purity, and sanctity. Those which are mine cannot represent "I". If we try and understand 'I', we need to be practicing its quality. But today, it is not about knowing yourself but telling you that you only manifest soul. Soul talks of spiritual intelligence.

Our body, temple of soul, creates our Bodily intelligence, we call it Physical quotient, physical status. Body represents tangible intelligence which we can feel and can take care. Taking care of body is again about awareness and creating choices of keeping it healthy. First what we eat. Nutrition gives every cell the strength to grow and function. Food plays a major role to keep ourselves fit and fine. Knowing nutrition, having balanced diet takes care of regaining energy to make our body function properly. Food plays a major role to keep our body fit and fine. All of us know what to eat, what not to eat. We know eating makes our soul and spirit calm and energetic. Right kind of food taking without any temptation helps us to sleep well. The energy requires for digestion during night is where the magic of wise nutrition is. It is the energy too we can save for the next day, if we eat moderately and timely during evening. Take dinner by 8 PM max and eat moderate. This will help digestive system work properly and also will not use excessive energy, which may make you feel drained. We eat without intelligence when we are exhausted, tired. We think of controlled eating but we do not make that happen. Overeating is causing our spirit restless and we loose energy. We should always take note of wise nutrition which is nothing but making us aware about choices of food we need to make.

Let us also know about "Regular Exercise". This is required with wise nutrition. Working out 5-6 days a week keep us healthy. Exercise is nothing but helps cells to rejuvenate and supply of abundant oxygen happens to all cells of body. Exercise should also include muscle toning and building muscle mass. Regular exercise is nothing but compliments wise nutrition. Getting up early and spending one and half hour for your body by stretching, muscle toning, and weight lifting keeps your body work with enormous energy. Basic metabolism is maintained which helps us utilizing our energy in a better way.

To enhance physical quotient, also we need to allow us for proper resting. Resting is nothing, but making us reloaded with all energy to make our days bright. It is energizing your all senses, making you focus more. Hence go for cheek ups understand changes in body. Prevention will help us sustain. If we neglect our body, we always tend to become sick. What will happen to our heart then?? Can we Love, can we think purity? We cannot develop patience, love, compassion. What will happen to our Emotional Intelligence? Keeping promise to you is integrity. If you fail to help a healthy health with some sacrifices, what promise you can make to others, to the society. If we neglect our body, what happens to soul, our spirit? Our energy which is our spirit will not be comfortable being in that body. Development of energy, strength will get hindered. Physical self mastery is a foundation of keeping your mind and spirit intact.

Let understand our mind, which is Intelligent Quotient. Our intelligence is nothing but practicing and doing. Mind, of enormous strength can be made stronger by 'continuous study' 'Making yourself aware", 'thinking out of the box; "do what you learn"

"Continuous Study:

Today being complacent of where we are, is actually killing ourselves. In today's scenario, with a continuous change in technology and others, our job nature may become redundant and we are out of all our comfort zone. Continuous study which is related to your area of work or something new will make us know about new things of the world. It will only help us adapt, change and making us at par with today's requirement. Study journals, researches, fiction, non-fiction. Creating library is an asset which you can leave a legacy. Invest in study, invest your resources to build library. Read books, have a systematic study for at least 60 minutes a day will make you shine. The asset which will value you is your books, the best friend, and the best companion. It will never ditch you; will always be with you to help you make choices.

"Making yourself Aware: Thinking Out of the Box:

Awareness creates your choices. The gap of stimulus and response is only get widened by being aware. Thinking differently, moreover keeping choices for a particular problem is only about assuring result. The adaptability, being a catalyst of change is the pathway of thinking differently. Being aware will simply help us making our decision explicit. Writing diaries, journals, putting observations on a piece of paper is actually making our choices known to us, it becomes visible. Writing observation does altogether help us analyze. Another way to analyze self is feedback seeking. Feedback positive, negative will only help us being aware. Here I would like to narrate of story of a boy, who once went to a STD shop to make a local telephone call. He borrows coin from the shopkeeper and dialed a number. The shopkeeper closely watched him. The boy was talking to a lady:

Boy : Madam, can you please employ me to take care of your garden.

Lady : No man, I have already kept someone for the same job.

Boy : Madam, I am ready to do the job even if I am paid half of the salary the present boy is getting.

Lady : But the existing chap is doing pretty good and I am happy.

Boy : Then keep me for your house. I will help cleaning your house. I will do it for tree.

Lady : Please forgive me, I don't require your service.

The boy started smiling and kept the phone down. Shopkeeper offered him a job. He said the shopkeeper, now I don't require any job. Thanks for offering me a job. The shopkeeper see surprised and asked "You were pleading for a job two minute before".

Boy : Actually I was finding that whether I am doing my job perfect by or not. I was talking to my employer. She is happy.

Hence feedback is important. You give your best, the whole world will support you.

Learning by doing:

Learning, being aware is in our hand but what is implemented that is actual learning. So many philosophies, ideologies, perfections, rituals of no use if not practiced, or not done. We learn not to say lie, but if we lie, then no point learning that fact. We all have same inheritance; the joy is how we use our learning.

Intelligent Quotient is all about continuous study, making yourself aware, thinking out of the box and taking feedback. A focus of continuous improvement will make this sharpened.

Emotional Quotient:

If our body and mind start working without heart, it will work like a machine. It is again self awareness, self motivation, self thought process. We are driven by heart, it keeps us being empathetic towards seeing & doing. It is again about

"Self awareness". "How will you be Enthusiastic"; know "Your Daily regulating skills, know how "You being Understanding" etc..

We talked about self awareness, self awakening, knowing yourself. Mental mastery will be automatically attained. Knowing self, is the most difficult task. We will talk about it when we will discuss about inside out approach. But not being reactive will actually help us analyze where we are good at.

Being enthusiastic always is how you really manifest your thought process. Being motivated is only making right choices. Understanding priorities and acting on it.

Daily regulation will only make someone perfect. It is how you set your priorities and regulate yourself. The Practice of daily regulation will actually make us perfect and improve skill set.

Being understanding is all about communication and sociability. When we communicate, the mode should be moreover a listener and being listened or create win win situation. Someone opens heart if he/she is not heard but 'Listened'.

Sharpening Emotional Quotient always takes a back seat. Ignoring EQ or procrastination will always lead poor intelligence by heart. Stress, trauma, tension reduces this intelligence. We know about "SEROTONIN" As a neurotransmitter, serotonin helps to relay messages from one area of the brain to another. Because of the widespread distribution of its cells, it is believed to influence a variety of psychological and other body functions. Of the approximately 40 million brain cells, most are influenced either directly or indirectly by serotonin. This includes brain cells related to mood, sexual desire and function, appetite, sleep, memory and learning, temperature regulation, and some social behavior. Increase of Serotonin increases with happiness. It had got an active and passive effect. You smile, do a right thing will increase your serotonin level, also as well will increase serotonin who has received your kindness. Hence we should think of increasing our self immune system. Our EQ gets diminished or reduced if we do not make ourselves prone to these tensions, stresses etc. We need to win ourselves to win people heart.

We often lose focus of our soul. We forget the from which we are created. We lose strength of our "Soul", our "Spirit". Intelligences of all kind is only by-product of our "Spiritual Intelligence". The strength within, is the power of soul. Spirit only changes it's body, hence the truth lies with soul. Replacing "Bad thoughts with good thoughts" "Always feeling good" and "spreading love empathy, purity", is all about how we can enhance our Spiritual Intelligence.

"Replacing bad thought with good thought": our life is full of experiences. The work we do, we receive the result, which manifests ritual. The rite of us is nothing but the result of our work, our "Karma" in Sanskrit. The observance of rituals emanates through outer deeds and our thoughts. If somebody has hatred as a culture, he will manifest the same and will get the result in return. But how we could enhance the spiritual intelligence, it is nothing but replacing those bad thoughts with good one. The result of our deeds will always come in our way, but we can only make us think good so that it does not manifest hatred, anger etc in our daily life. We know we will get back what we have done, but we can be very sure of our future of being positive and powerful thinker.

By "Always feeling good" :

We should feel good always, feeling good will attract good. But this cannot happen until and unless we strengthen our soul, our spirit. Abundance of positive thought will create destiny and more thinking good will help make us ready to face any adversity. Always feeling good is about practice, but practice this whole heartedly and make this a very conscious effort.

Spreading love, empathies, purity...

Spirit is pure. The enhancement of spiritual power in positive way can only happen by practicing purity. Purity is the quality of soul. But we make it corrugated by Anger, frustration etc. If we believe purity, practice purity, we transform energy and create energy within and surround us.

The spark inside you – You are inside you

Your subconscious mind, a spark within us, the strength of us, It makes us aware. Simple part of mind, never sleeps, never takes rest.

We are in a journey for destiny. The journey is all about me, inside me, outside world cannot control it. We can see which we want to see. A painter not necessarily good with colour and pencil, but he needs to see things he wants to paint. Conscious mind and subconscious mind, The parts of brain, not two functions but actually makes us behave. Conscious gives us rational thinking, subconscious gives us principles. It we start talking about merits of subconscious mind we actually will understand the "SPARK" we possess. It's just to know how to make it strong.

A magnet with its strength on, can take 10 times load but without it's strength, can't even take load of a paper or it can't make the paper stabilized. Subconscious mind is all about strength with has to be maintained. It's another mind in our mind. Conscious mind, thinks, sees, does, drives. But subconscious takes the massage while conscious thinks and does. Subconscious creates, restores our destiny, our future. Its up to me, what would I like to say my subconscious to restore. Your conscious does thing with anger, hatred, your subconscious will record and the same will happen to you. This is simply law of attraction. We do things, we create beliefs, our parents, and society teaches us something. The false belief will only make us mediocre in thought process. Hence we should learn to stop occupying false belief. Otherwise we will always be apprehensive about new things and will refrain ourselves from making better choices.

Conscious gives order, we do. It is visible everywhere in our life. Captain tells us how to play, orders. Trainers' orders to do exercise but the thought which got created are in subconscious mind makes our life. If we see our mind is a garden and the seed of thought through conscious mind is harvested in the garden. The seed will yield result which is our next action. If we do good, subconscious will manifest good. Subconscious is rich soil, Whatever, good bad seed is harvested, It will attract the similar result.

Hence we need to learn, how to think and act. Conscious being objective in nature will always be driven though objects. But subconscious is subjective. It creates feeling, manifests or portrays good or bad result.

We talked about faith, auto suggestion, filtered thoughts, power thinking – all are manifestation of how we nurture our subconscious mind. It is always working, it is always creating, but who controls, it's again your thought which is inside you. Subconscious is the answer of all problems. Since we only harvested the problem and related result will only be for us, not for anyone else. Hence using your thought to search answer of all odds, is a learning which we understood.

Good thoughts v/s. bad thoughts we need to differentiate. The result, outcome, is in our hand. Subconscious does not understand why, it only records. It does not understand law, but only driven through principles.

To quote here, why different people behave in different way towards a common stimulus? You are inside you. Your subconscious recording may drive you to act differently. Response towards a Movie will be different for two individuals. This is only because of the impression which subconscious mind has. The principles, logic, irrationality of our subconscious will take one common thing in different perspective. It is nothing but what is impressed in the same will express out. It does control our body, it does heal our wound. The principles of regulation we understand will only be the outcome. We chose how our subconscious will behave.

Hence we, all human beings, can determine our destiny. The World is waiting for us to have experience, no one creates except us. Everything starts from us and hence the outer world created. Here would like to quote our incident which generally happens with people. One day I couldn't able to find my watch during power cut and it was complete darkness, I could see street lights are on, and thought of these lights can help me to find out my watch. But unfortunately those lights couldn't help me, the darkness around me was my block of mind, it was nothing but I just would have searched for a source of light and got my problem resolved. The watch was just lying on the bed nearby but it took me hours to find out.

It was me who was supposed to come out with solution; no one will come and eradicate my problem. We find a place beautiful, since it makes us delighted, it is only the feeling of us make things better and worse. But whenever we are in sorrow, in stress, in agony, we lose our calm, we lose our power. God's picture, idol etc are depicted with more than one hand sometime. We call it God with multiple hands. But it is nothing, the hands symbolizes the power of the divine soul. Power of the soul is actually make us think. The soul has a power to love, power of forgiveness, power of beauty, power of abundance, power of kindness- humility. We only are responsible to retain or deplete these powers of soul. When we deplete these, we search solutions of problems outside. We understand or presume God will come and help us, but we forget the divinity inside in lieu of powers has been already reduced. This is "I", the power are in "I". But we say "I" is a name, "I" is a professional designation. "I" is a relation; "I" is a stature. But it is not "I", these are 'mine'. The powers within "I" make us approach inside out. Most of us are blaming outside World for everything happening with us. It is 'me' who has to start, think that "I" am responsible for all happenings of my life.

Chapter 5

FAILURE IS NEVER FINAL . . .

Road Blocks, hindrances of dreams, failing to achieve dream, or we actually fail to dream!!!. Beliefs, societal structure, experiences, etc.. all are influenced by outer World. Outside us, whatever happens; is not easy to control comparing things to be controlled inside us. The simple answer is 'you'.

We think of luck, luck is made, luck is created, luck is a wish. Thought, energy, vibration one can create. We are born, will grow up and die. We are born from a dot, the dot determines our body colour, our hair, our physical qualities, our nails….. It is created, but these are beyond our imagination. Luck is the way you think, you do, and you are going to get the same in return. You can only create your luck. Thinking unlucky is only stopping you being lucky. It is very simple. You make it, create it. Whatever we do, we get result here only.

<u>We get stuck with our thought or belief:-</u>

We have seen in previous chapters, how we feel from childhood to adulthood. We know the stimulus available outside us, some very common, some seldom appears. Our relatives, friends, their thought and beliefs also impact our thought process. They say, this is right way, you should obey this since it is being followed, being with God and do all rituals to satisfy God, if someone ditches you the same needs to be done with him. These thought process becomes imposition sometimes and we do follow knowingly, unknowingly. But if we try and understand that all these beliefs is nothing but manifested from different experiences of life. Those experiences have taken place only in outside World and we got influenced with those experiential stimulus. If, something happened to us, we immediately think and be judgmental….we often think this is because of these factors or this is because of this person or so. We immediately or always play a blame game and wait for that external factor to get rectified at earliest, if not, we adjust and live on.

But now close your eyes. See what was told, what was experienced and what was in result. We will find a common factor in all these; is how we perceived the experience, the result has come out accordingly. The estimation of thought only has created result. Another factor which was immediately came to mind, if I wouldn't have done this, this wouldn't have happened. Here lies the 'UNDERSTANDING'. It starts from 'I' and ends with 'I'. If I is capable enough to understand what internal strength, anyone can be developed to fight out these external stimulus, then actual introspection will happen. Being influenced or getting influenced is all about your internal strength, not external factors. The thoughts and beliefs are only with us, which will manifest result.

<u>We get stuck because of unawareness</u>:

We have also seen in previous chapters that awareness only precedes choice and choice precedes result. We also saw, choice is only factor between stimulus and action. We also have seen how to expand the gap of choice and stimulous, so that we can predict result.

Unaware of what? Unaware of tomorrow? Unaware of life or unaware of self? Need to think these answers. The answer comes from almost everyone that "how someone knows about tomorrow or future" or how someone predict result"? But we are only responsible for us. It is we, create our tomorrow. The basic unawareness is about self. We don't know us, the potential, the quality within. We are always judged by people around us. People say we act. Self non awareness is the biggest road block. We know, all of us are born with some birth right, but our entire destiny is different. Now the question is how we can know us, or how we can create our future. Dr. Dyer expressed is his book "Power of Intention" a statement from old testament "As a man thinketh so is he". Think positively and you will produce positive result.

The positive you attract to your life. You attract positive, you get positive. That is where we need to find out our inner strength. If we think what is not there in our life we will get nothing, but if we think we intend to have xyz, the same will manifest. It is about thought process. All, what you attract you get. Rhonda Byrne's "Secret" says it better, "Like attracts Like"

It's not about what "I" don't want it's about what "I" want. All of us is majorly mistaken on this. Hence we create thought and we create future.

The unawareness lies with us, we have all strength. It is just a vibration of positive thought, makes our life Heaven.

<u>We get stuck because of our experience of life :-</u>

The experience of life, wherever we are today, we all have experiences which are mostly felt and seen. Human, which mostly seen and felt generally remembers. We say, learning is all about doing. Physical existence of experience plays a major role towards remembrance. If God thinks, seeing today's depleted souls, I can't create anymore, since it doesn't work, will it be good for life ! It's same with us, if we get succumbed by our negative experiences we can never come up and live life. Experience is references to learn, we need to actually categorically understand the best thing happened. Analyzing better, will surely give us a thought, what we attracted, so is happened. If we say, things doesn't work of me, it will never work. But if we say, things will work in abundance for me, it will definitely work. It is just a thought with purpose.

Getting stuck is very simple, but getting abundance is simplest, only to attract good.

<u>We get stuck to use Energy:</u>

Energy is vibration, the wave. The size, frequency of wave creates the impact. The whole World is energy field. Our Own energy level is what is felt by us and other people. Higher energy always nullifies lower energy. If we want to understand energy sources the sources may be metal energy, sound energy, light energy, thought energy and spiritual energy.

Metal energy is felt whenever metal is touched and the energy very low in metal, since vibration is low. But when a wave of sound created, it creates a vibration and we generally feel the energy what sound waves are creating. But light moves faster than sound. The energy of light waves is much stronger than sound waves, because of the speed. The light waves create energy which is used in our daily life. But the energy is tremendous.

All of us understand these energies which are felt, seen. We can reduce, amend, and increase the energy these sources are creating. But being human we also create energy and to be very precise, thought energy is created every second. We know, our mind can run fast and it can reach anywhere within a fraction of second. This also creates an energy field. If we are aware, we can see this or feel. Thoughts of any nature is impacting our actions and also impacting our body. You feel low when you are frustrated, stressed, in agony, in tension, abused or shouted etc. But you feel good when you smile, laugh, love. If means, the purity of thought, which creates the field of energy, make us feel low or high. Feeling Low or high is all about energy we create.

Above all, pure the spirit is; the energy is high. We have seen good spirits who emanates abundance of energy, generally in monks, saints, sages. The purity or divinity of spirit will always create energy. It is the most powerful energy source. If we are connected to source from where we have come, the Divinity, love, purity of the spirit will always create abundance of energy. The spirits with ego, hatred, will always emanate low vibration. If we quote an example of a classroom of a school, children are making noise, shouting …….. but as soon as teacher comes in, the noise reduces but doesn't stop completely. The teacher bangs wooden duster on the table and also shouts not to make noise. The noise gets reduced to some extent further. It is energy of that sound and teacher being senior, somehow could create an energy which made the noise reduced. It is same in any gathering or assembly, when the speaker gets up on the stage, noise reduces without any bang. The reason is, the energy of inheritance of the speaker nullifies the noise of the audience. But during discourses when saints, sages or master comes, the environment becomes pure and tranquility prevails. It is just because of abundance of spiritual energy the master carried nullifies all noise of the audience. Manifestation of Spiritual energy starts from thought process. The thought inside us is driven through intelligences. The spiritual intelligence creates spiritual energy. We are from a source, getting connected to that source is making us strong and we can feel omnipotence of divinity. Which we generally misinterpret by feeling saying God resides inside us. The energy originated from divinity is the most powerful one.

The question is how to increase energy level of self. What will help us enhance our energy level? We know it starts from every individual, outside World doesn't influence this at all.

Firstly we would understand how we think. "Thought Clarity" is very much important. Being conscious about thoughts coming in every time is actually the first step of thinking good. The low energy thought if replaced by high energy thought, automatically energy field is enhanced. This is simple to listen, simple to hear but simplest to do. Only thought is to do it. Be very careful for every situation. Carry your "RITE". The thought creates "RITE". It someone loves people, will create RITE which is full of love, it someone being violent, will create same rite. The essence is the rite which got created will emanate energy. Always think to pursue right kind of thought. Replace bad thoughts immediately with good thoughts. The consciousness, always thinking well will bring in "Thought Clarity and in turn create abundance of energy.

We know how to choose. Calm mind, pure mind will always think better, chooses better. Hence "MEDIATION" is essential. It's a ritual. It's a practice. So many method of meditation is available today. But every method talks about attainment of peaceful mind. It is nothing but rejuvenation your mind to think better. Relax your mind for 10-15 mins a day in a calm place to start with. It will create energy; it will help us choose actions of each stimulus. Hence we are more controlled, thought more controlled.

Take right kind of diet. The diet, "Food habit" helps us to run basic metabolism of our body. Timely food, right food is actively helping us produce energy to work. To work efficiently fundamentally we need to take care of our food habit. We discussed this in our previous chapters.

Do not get indulged in "Energy Wasters". Watching television, gossiping, sleeping etc are not going to help us build energy. Choosing right "People around" will bring in energy in our life. We have seen; if we talk to someone who has better command on language, will automatically motivate us speaking better. If we see, someone very conscious about his health, it compels us to think that we should also lead a disciplined life. It is nothing the energy field, the right acquaintance create; will always help us enhance the same.

Quitting is always impacting in longer run, where in the pain is very momentary.

Roadblockes, suffering, problems makes us strong.

Chapter 6

CORE IDEOLOGY OF LIFE

Now here we need to understand the definite path of leading a life. We need to understand the ideology of leading life. Ideology of making life meaningful and action oriented. All have been given the same resource in life and no one has been given less or more resources of leading life. God has given us everything in abundance and equal. We have seen various aspects of leading a life starting from achieving Physical Mastery to Mental Mastery.

Purpose of Life:

Purpose of Life is Life of Purpose. The agenda of life depends on WHY you are there and HOW you are going to accomplish and WHAT you are supposed to do. The essence of life lies with the PURPOSE.

We call PURPOSE is the Core Ideology of life. Purpose makes life go. We all are seeing different human beings surrounded and think of how this PURPOSE makes them moving, make their life go on. The PURPOSE understanding or clarity of Life's purpose is where we should spend time and understand the Core.

"Core ideology is the fundamental reason of living beyond just living daily – a guiding principle of life, which will always remain constant."

The Core makes us different. We know the guiding principles which has to be remembered and followed everyday basis. The will power and conviction only will help these driven regularly. Purpose is clear, we just need to stimulate change and lead a life which has a destiny.

We see Core Ideology of famous personalities in their biography. We see a definite purpose of their life. If peace and tranquility is the Purpose, it has been followed all across their life. Martin Luthar King, Mahatma Gandhi has showcased these throughout. It means whatever comes across, but the purpose always remains constant.

Importance of PURPOSE – The Core Ideology:

It's a perpetual guiding principle of our life. One may have one PURPOSE; one may have more than one PURPOSES. To understand it more clearly you need to look in your Soul. The spirit and the understanding the power of spirit will help us derive the Core Ideology. The guiding principles, which we need to follow everyday whatever we do. It remains core always. It helps us:

- Think with clarity:
- Clarity in thought brings peace. Problems/roadblocks are learnings all through.
- Do the job with predetermining result, Do the job more clearly, Help make others life Purposeful.

Core ideologies are constants of life and they are never changeable. Be Spiritual, be Truthful, be at Service always. The ideologies are to be inherited, nurtured.

Being spiritual:

Spiritual is not only about being God faithful. It is creating serenity, love, foregiveness, trust and energy. Serenity is being calm under any stressful circumstances. If we want to understand stress, it should be always taken as result of our non awareness. Non awareness create stress, we create anxiety, we create dilemma. Being serene at all circumstances is being aware of the reasons of stress. The reasons will only help us to reach to the answers. Believing yourself is actually the answer. It will create and spread love all around. Love with all good intentions, love with heart in it is actually being spiritual. It is love towards your surroundings, love your ownself, love your acquaintances, love your job, love your all beings which makes you live, make you spiritual. The strength of spirit will only get enhanced by loving someone or something., not by hatred.

Forgiving is another strength which has to be developed. Being in this world and always fighting for existence is challenge to all of us. It is tough to forgive always, since we all are driven through our emotions, instincts. But always forgiving will only make us live for others which is nothing but practicing spirituality. The essence of service, the essence of being with someone during his troublesome days is all about practicing spirituality. Forgive sin, forgive pain, forgive distrust, forgive humiliation, forgive hatred, forgive all odd which make you sorrow. The essence of bringing joy, in-spite of all odds is foregiveness. Have trust with yourself. The trust for you will make all your surroundings trust you. It always reciprocates. Trust will always bring in trust. The spirituality is practiced by bringing back trust of others into our life. Trust without all inhibitions is spirituality which will manifest forgiveness.

Our thoughts create energy. The whole universe is an energy field. Positive thought always emanante energy. If you are in anguish, you are hating, you generally feel down, but whenever you listen to some motivational speech, you feel energetic. When we do a job which we like mostly, we feel energetic doing that job. Energy needs to be maintained throughout. Hence remaining positive, remaining good will always help us maintain the energy.

Preserve core ideology of life. It gives us purpose. It helps us move, it helps us learn.

Being Truthful:

It is to you. Being truthful means, being truthful to self which is actually practicing spirituality. The main challenge of someone is to know himself. By being truthful you choose the path of knowing yourself. Whatever our action may be, it will definitely have reaction. Learning from those results and acknowledging the mistakes is only practicing truthfulness. Maintain truthfulness against all odds is preserving the core.

Being at Service Always:

You become the same to others which you expect to become with you. We spend our life for self, but being at service to others will always bring in happiness in abundance in your life. Since what you do you get the same in return! Make yourself available for society, make yourself available for your family, make yourself available for your friends, make yourself available for your colleagues. Let the world find you when it requires your presence. Making yourself available will only ensure you being at service to others.

The core ideology is not just your core, it should be the core of your family and friends. If you make them believe, you can only practice the same and it will remain constant.

By preserving core we can stimulate our development and progress. Stimulating self development is always changeable. It will change with time, it will change with learning, it will change always. Self development keeping the core----will only gain momentum and we create progress in life.

Stimulating Development:

By Learning: Every moment of our life is learning. Learning by study, learning by seeing, learning by experiencing, learning by doing, learning of all nature changes in different phases of life. Inquisitiveness only will stimulate learning. Learning make awareness and awareness will only create result.

By adapting change: Every moment change is inevitable in human life. Change in weather condition, change in people behavior, change in self understanding, change in all aspect is mandatory. Resisting change or adapting change, we need to choose. This choice only will make life grow and stimulate development.

Resisting change—It results in no growth of human potential. People resist change for certain belief, prejudice, mental block. Cursing luck or God is the only outcome they receive. They only become roadblock of their aspirations.

Adapting change is only developing required thought process.

By developing proper life Style:

It is only about utilizing resources of life. Utilising time is very very important. How you can have more time will only lead you to achieve result. We will see various aspects of achieving self mastery also. The spirit of achieving self mastery is only about utilizing your resources. When strategy is multiplied by resource we achieve result.

Stimulating development, stimulating progress is where we should focus, but the Core needs to be maintained or else progress will not manifest a feeling of achievement.

Chapter 7

BE READY TO ACT

Learning by doing, is the actual learning. We see things and learn, we listen and learn, and we do and learn. We know what power thinking is. A power thinker is always ready to act. Success is never final, failure makes us strong. Don't think that other will come and do your quota of job. It's you who needs to act upon.

We know choices; the right choice will yield better result. We make choices and act, it's called Pro-action. But when we instantly act without much of choices, we react. We have seen awareness only precedes choice. To act, we really have to think about enabling our choices of life. To act, which is actually playing your role, but if that role playing is only about doing something; will not make us master, we will be master my constant practicing.

Building Mental Mastery and Knowledge:

We know, practice makes a man perfect. A particular skill gets developed and we achieve mastery practicing it for Ten Thousand hours. We also know mastery is nothing about putting 20% effort to get 80% result. We have seen the basic differentiation between hard worker and smart worker. It's all about making yourself master of act. Mediocrity is easy to achieve, it is very common in today's world.

We all have certain beliefs, certain perceptions about self. When we perceive something about own, we try to undermine our own self. We think, if I fail, if I can't do this, if I am not able to cope up ….. etc. etc. The self understanding, if mediocre, always brings us down, this is because of

1. Low self belief or low self esteem
2. Lack of will power

3. Mediocre people surrounded by
4. Reference points not worked upon
5. Lack of knowledge
6. Self goal or aim if not fixed.

Low Self belief or low self esteem:

We often do not know ourselves. We think this is not my cup of tea. I cannot perform this job. Here we need to take an oath. An oath of Self realization. Only a shift of thought process will help us analyze the potential within us. We have enormous strength, which is just needed to be known and explored.

Lack of Will power :-

Will power is something which is very uncommon in people. But everyone in this world knows about this. It we talk about quitting smoking or quitting drug, no strength in this World can do it for you, it you yourself do not want to get rid of this habit. Only our will shall work. But the required energy to execute is not available with people commonly. The energy will only get generated within us through clean thought process and spiritual thinking. Strong determination and will power will only help us see and act differently.

Improve your surroundings (Surrounded by Mediocre People) :-

What human being see, hear, they follow. It is common for every living human being. Being human, what we see, witness perceives all as truth and starts believing in. Mediocre people, mediocre thought, mediocre surroundings, influence our thought process. Put life up to achieving some goal. Commitment requires action, committed to a goal, will definitely put us in pressure of putting action to make it happen. Life without pressure without commitment becomes monotonous and boring. Now how to put pressure on self? "Be cautious about Procrastination". Procrastination looks very simple and very common. We generally do not understand how we do it. Simple regular jobs at office also kept for tomorrow, which would have been an important job for today. We lack that understanding of delaying will automatically cut short our time, the asset, commonly available with all of us. We sometime do it unintentionally.

But problem lies, even if after understanding the ill effects of procrastination we do not get committed do it. Hence being aware will automatically help us choose. Procrastination, generally has been not worked out, hence gets into habit. Habit of procrastination is what we should reject.

"It's impossible to fail completely and it's impossible to succeed perfectly" – Schuller.

It is also recommended to be Affirmative. Being affirmative is nothing, simple turn around your thought. A common question, "Am I be able to perform this task? I do not have skill set". Being affirmative "I will leran the skill and complete this task". In our daily life we all can practice affirmation. Affirmation, positive thought, all come hand on hand. We human being just to believe in this and practice it.

Reference Points not worked upon :-

Another reason to fail, not having reference points. We discussed concept of reference points in one of the previous chapters. Our Mother is always kind; she is always referred for Kindness. Hence Mother, her thought process can be understood, followed to become kind. The pain she takes the sacrifices she makes for being kind to her child and her family. When we see all good practices, as a ritual we should follow this, practice this. What we say when it's our turn to become kind; we get into blame game, we indulge in saying that the other person should showcase kindness, since the fault is his. We fail to become kind, we fail to sacrifice; we fail to bear pain, which is always temporary. We have seen reference points and importance of reference points in our life. We human beings believe what is seen. Still we fail to work upon the basics of

a. Being Positive
b. Being in controlled thought
c. Being Committed
d. Being result oriented.
e. Being empathetic etc.

Here we should talk of rituals. Rituals are practices, practices in due course becomes ritual. When discipline becomes our ritual, we generally do all tasks without being monitored or without much of mental stress. We take an example of brushing teeth in the morning; do we need to really remember to do it, or it happens automatically whenever we get up. Another ritual is to get early. We make commitment to leave bed early and we follow the same. In spite of some problems continuous practice will be able to make it. Ritual makes our behavior highly structured. It we look at different parts of our life, we find that habits of certain nature make our life possible. Making life possible is by building routine, discipline. We talked of disciplined food habits, taking nutritious food on time are all about a ritual which we should follow.

Lack of Knowledge :

Awareness is required for making choice. Awareness comes from knowledge. Knowledge gaining or continuous enhancement of knowledge is helping human being sustain change. Change is inevitable. Change is the truth. Every moment we are experiencing change. Being orthodox to change will not help us grow, will surely make us inanimate. Knowledge of change or change adaptability is absolute truth, makes us go. Suggested followings steps to make us up to date or will help us enhance knowledge:-

A) Study rgularly
B) Train yourself or attain seminars
C) Implement learning
D) Be open to accept

It is recommended for everyone to study regularly. Books are the best friend. They are with you always in need; the learning will only help us see in a different way. All change to adapt is only can be practiced by the usage of knowledge. Until and unless we know different choices, we are not able to see things differently. Seeing differently is nothing but creating point of view, making one self aware.

Attending training sessions, seminars happens with people in different organizations. But implementation of learning is often dormant. Being cognitive and implementation of learning makes everyone different. 'Purpose of life is a life of purpose'. Change adaptability, knowledge implementation is all about being purposeful. Purpose creases direction and hence we act.

<u>Self goal and aim is not fixed</u> :-

Purpose, a definite one, will help creating aim. Achieving aim will only be manifested with a definite purpose and a clear cut roadmap. Inspiring self, regularly, will only help us stick to the aim. We know, when we drive at night, we can see only 200-250 meters through the headlight of the vehicle, but we know we are destined for several thousand kilometers to so. Here we only have purpose and a clear road to reach destination. All of us are aware of the same truth, but still we fail to achieve our goal or aims of life. Since we don't trust us, since we do not have faith in us; when the purpose gets defeated, we run away from the truth. Truth only will create action. Vision thru purpose is mentioned here as truth. Vision doesn't come automatically; it is always aligned with purpose. Vision is created, crafted and implemented. A purposeful life will only come with a definite purpose.

Recommended steps for reaching our goal –

    a.   Fix a goal
    b.   Give it a deadline
    c.   Be committed to deadline
    d.   Everyday measure improvement
    e.   Inculcate intelligence and quality in purpose.
    f.   Reach the crooning stage of achieving goal.

All steps seems to be very simple, to be precise all of these are simple, only we need to act on it.

Action creates result; every action will have its reaction. It is upto us which reaction we want. Hence we become self leader. Self leadership is necessary.

<u>Self Leadership</u> :-

Everything starts at you. The rituals, the steps, the suggestions are all about how you lead yourself.

It includes:

    a. Physical Mastery
    b. Mental Mastery

Listing out steps of physical mastery is very easy, but the rituals of physical mastery you need to follow, you have to have that willpower. Mental mastery starts from your thought. Your thought consciousness will only lead you to achieve mental mastery. All intelligences we mentioned is previous chapters are driven towards achieving Mental Mastery only.

Self leadership is what has to be developed to showcase people leadership or mass leadership. It applies everywhere in our life. It influences our daily life. It influences our family, it influences our work place environment, and it influences our social environment. It is a paradigm of moving our life ahead with a purpose. The choices are with every one of us.

Chapter 8

CROWNING STAGE

Fulfillment of achievement is crowning for us. We have seen in history, in various dynasties all crowing was celebrated, the energy of that celebration, creates a leader to lead. This is what the glory of success is. Every one of us dream of this stage. All of us are here to achieve our goal. Where life we do our best to reach our destiny. The destiny is only being created by us. Hence the joy of achievement is also of us.

To reach to this stage we have seen series of roadblocks. The roadblocks, the stoppers are actually created by God. He wants to understand whether we are very sure of reaching here. He will make us hurt, he will make us think, if we have taken a right decision of investing our time to sacrifice. These roadblocks are just to make us stick to our priorities and pay all price to reach to the stage of achievement.

We have started our journey with

1. Energetic Thinking: The thought process which makes us powerful. The energy of thoughts, the belief of thought.
2. Power of Faith. Faith is in the basics of all achievement. An idea, turns into faith and the faith with powerful thought process make our dream fulfilled. We know and also seen how our thought process and action changes in different Phases of life.
3. Different Phases of Life: All Phases of life are having its own identity and importance. Sticking to our priorities is the lesson which we need to adopt and learn. We have also learnt how to.
4. Influence ourselves: What we have as birth rights and equal in all of us. How we can be self motivators and live to attain destined goal. With all understanding we also understood.

5. How we should act: The action or implementation of all learnings. The joy of achievement lies in action. Above all, our learning, experiences started from a dream. It's all about self inspiration; it's all about how we understand our actions and how we are focused on goal. Determine your goal of life. The dream to fulfill, definite and specific goals are pathways to reach to that final goal. Spend time to:

Make your life's mission Statement

"I am here to spread Love, Knowledge and Energy. I am here to be grateful for everything I have"

A mission statement for our own life, it seems very simple. But all of us miss it actually. The statement which will create your ways to reach your destination is your Mission statement. Whatever your ability to visualize your life, your desire will help you make your mission statement. Visualize your house, the place you want to be, the person you want to be. We fail to visualize because of our experiences. If we would like to be an athlete and during the first competition you fumbled, couldn't make it, it will create an impression about self. The picture of self defeat will always hinder to think on the direction of actual self mastery.

The picture of failure will always dominate to see ourselves ahead of the fear. But self mastery is all about ignoring failure, visualize success by developing a self belief system. Self belief system, of you see yourself as champion of many athletic events, you should listen the ecstasy of people around. Huge applauses all around and you are joyful of achievement. Self belief and visualization is all about creating a success statement for yourself. The statement is all about what you want to be. Create a statement with measurable steps to it. Suggested to have followings in mind while you write your statement:

a. You see yourself as ......
b. You would like to do ....
c. You would like to achieve.........
d. The time you like to devote...........
e. Self evaluation mechanism to establish.

All though you need to be in your statement, deviation, diversion, circumstantial hindrances should take a back seat. Make a statement and live it..

Make an overall Goal and plan all steps :-

Goal which is measurable can be achieved, although realistic GOAL has a meaning:

G: Get

O: Opportunities

A: Avail and

L: Live

I see Goal is nothing but understanding opportunities and putting plans. Mission Statement derives Goal and Goal is achieved by planning the steps. Short term and Long Term Goals are only made possible through Plan and executing the Plan. Our Goal may have following understandings. You need to choose.

a. Goal for achieving self mastery
b. Materialistic Goal
c. Financial Goal
d. Goal for People

What is Goal for Achieving Self Mastery:

Make a list of to dos to achieve self mastery. Short term and long term (5-10 year) plan is essential to make. We have already seen so many ways and means to achieve Self Mastery- but the conviction is something we need to develop. Putting everything in your journal is very important.

Make a 5 year plan:

- Out of 5 Goals at least 2 has to be accomplished. E.g Establishing or Knowing Self potential or attaining Physical Mastery

Make a 10 Year Plan:

- Acquire specialization or knowledge.
- The books to study to acquire knowledge help you to achieve goal
- What kind of Seminars and Training to go through etc etc.

What is Materialistic Goal:

Its all about one's imagination. Imagination will only become burning desire when you will understand what kind of materialistic possession you want to have. All these should have a definite timeline. Writing all timeline in your journal will only make it happen. It should also be bifurcated in 5-10 year plan.

What is Financial Goal:

Clearly set the amount of Money you want to have after certain period of time. The same to written in your journal. What amount will give you a freedom and what kind of amount you want to posses and when?

What is Goal for People:

Live for yourself and live by giving it back to people. The thought of service, the patience of being with people, will help you accumulate more. The universal law say, what you give you get it back, will only happen if you have that mentality to share your services. You should also have plan for your family, for your children and also what services you can provide to human kind. Have a definite Road Map when you are able to go back to society to pay tribute and gain more in return.

Execute your plan and implement:

Execution of your plan, how small it may be, will only require commitment and sticking towards it. Commitment towards short term goal achievement is found to be easy and common in all human beings. But commitment towards long term goal often vanishes because of lack of commitment. Contemplation of hindrances towards making goal, facing challenges may cause non execution of goal. But viewing challenges as learning will only help us stick to the commitment. Commitment will always require action to get goals fulfilled.

Commitment is self discipline. Commitment comes from will power. Will power comes from within. Always being committed is tough for any human being. Short time achievements and keeping commitment for long term achievement is contradictory. Here comes will power, a strong will for being committed can only help us reach destination. Creating will take time; it has to be practiced religiously. We have talked of spiritual intelligence, the only way to bring in will power in our life, it's all about accumulating energy, the energy within will only creates will power.

Some small steps to keep our commitment burning:

A. Meditate Regularly: Meditation, the first step towards achieving concentration Concentrated effort will always take less time and always brings in efficiency in result. Concentration is all about bringing result and manifestation of success. Meditation is the key to practice concentration. Meditation is communication. Communicating with the source we emanate. Communication with our God is helping us gaining energy. It is believed, the purity of atmosphere, the tranquility of surroundings help us concentrate and communicate with God. When we close eyes, so many thought comes, if we stop them, will definitely result irritation. Hence the best way to meditate is to establish two way communication with our almighty. It is the process of understanding the existence of power and gathering that power to accumulate energy. The communication is all about creating will power, self mastery.

B. Writing Everyday Steps: We do so many things a day, some most important, some important, some less important, relatively compared to our goal setting. But can we avoid less important ones, no, and then what we need to do to make our daily goal successful. Hence suggested here to write and plan your daily steps. This will automatically help us filter out less important tasks. It will surely bring more clarity towards everything than being less effective in achieving daily goal.

C. Analyzing the Days activities before going to sleep: Very important and carries lots of influence towards fulfilling dreams. Analyzing and criticizing self makes us what we want to be. Suppose we planned to do 10 things and we could only do 8. But analyzing means, are those 8 most important or the steps what we had prioritized when we started the day. If the answer is yes, then we are on track and go for a lovely sleep. This is again a ritual, a ritual of self mastery and a ritual of getting all thought aligned with life's goal.

D. Be a self critic: Open to feedbacks. Ask people about your feedback. Be a self critic. Criticism is a negative feedback but being positive about self and criticizing your own doings will bring in clarity. This will firstly create thought process, will help us analyse what is right and what is wrong. Self conscious will get strengthened. Practice this regularly. Make this happen and bring in changes in life and the overall out look of life.

E. Reorganize energy for better result: Whatever we do, always is the manifestation of thought. Thought is energy, thought attracts thoughts and make an energy field. All possibilities exhibits energy and we feel contended when we feel that energy of fulfillment. Hence we need to learn reorganizing energy towards fulfillment of our task, job. Failure breaks energy, but success brings it back. We know tough time never last but tough people do…and failure brings in success. The learning from failures, the knowledge we gain out of failure, the conviction of success is all about reorganizing energy for fulfillment.

www.ingramcontent.com/pod-product-compliance
Lightning Source LLC
Chambersburg PA
CBHW020902310526
45786CB00018B/1551